The Names God Calls Us

Remembering Who We are to Our Creator

By
Kandra Albury

The Names God Calls Us

*Remembering Who We are
to Our Creator*

Copyright © 2024 by Kandra Albury

ISBN (979-8-9874925-9-8)

All rights reserved. No part of this book may be reproduced or transmitted in any form or by any means without written permission from the author.

Disclaimer: Various versions of the bible were utilized in the production of this text.
They are listed here as a reference, but this list is not definitive:
KJV, NKJV, NIV, MSG, NAS, & NLT

MTE Publishing
mtepublishing.com

Introduction:

God resorted to name calling first, but in the most beautiful and glorious ways!

God knows us by our birth names, however throughout scriptures, God's terms of endearment affirm and reinforce who we are before we ever came into existence.

This is a direct indication of WHO we are to our Creator.

As our relationship with our Creator evolves, we become intimately known, affectionately loved, and diligently pursued by God. He knows us better than we know ourselves.

After all, *He created us and calls us by name (Isaiah 43:1).*

One of my names growing up was "Pudda". It was given to me by my godmother's mom, Aunt Catherine, and I loved it!

As I reflect over my life and the names I have been called (good, bad, or indifferent), nothing compares to the names God bestowed upon me, first.

It is my hope that we will always remember that we are God's most prized creation as well as His beloved!

May we never forget the names God calls us, who He is to us, but most importantly, who we are to Him!

Dedication:

I dedicate this book to all of God's children. To you, me, us, them, every race, ethnicity, sexual orientation, political party — to all of us.

𝕬𝖈𝖈𝖊𝖕𝖙𝖊𝖉

To the praise of the glory of his grace, wherein he hath made us accepted in the beloved.

(Ephesians1:6 KJV)

Adopted by Christ

Having predestined us unto the adoption of children by Jesus Christ to himself, according to the good pleasure of his will.

(Ephesians 1:5 KJV)

Apple of His Eye

Keep me as the apple of your eye; hide me in the shadow of your wings

(Psalm 17:8 NIV)

Alive

But because of his great love for us, God, who is rich in mercy, made us alive with Christ even when we were dead in transgressions— it is by grace you have been saved.

(Ephesians 2:4-5 NIV)

Ambassadors

We are therefore Christ's ambassadors, as though God were making his appeal through us. We implore you on Christ's behalf: Be reconciled to God.

(2 Corinthians 5:20 NIV)

𝕭𝖊𝖑𝖔𝖛𝖊𝖉

Beloved, I wish above all things that thou mayest prosper and be in health, even as thy soul prospereth.

(3 John 1:2 KJV)

𝔅lessed

Blessed shalt thou be when thou comest in, and blessed shalt thou be when thou goest out.

(Deuteronomy 28:6 KJV)

Branches

"I am the vine; you are the branches. If you remain in me and I in you, you will bear much fruit; apart from me you can do nothing.

(John 15:5 NIV)

Children of God

Dear friends, now we are children of God, and what we will be has not yet been made known. But we know that when Christ appears, we shall be like him, for we shall see him as he is.

(1 John 3:2 NIV)

Chosen Generation

But you are a chosen race, a royal priesthood, a holy nation, a people for God's own possession, so that you may proclaim the excellencies of Him who has called you out of darkness into His marvelous light.

(1 Peter 2:9 NIV)

Citizens of Heaven

But we are citizens of heaven, where the Lord Jesus Christ lives. And we are eagerly waiting for him to return as our Savior.

(Philippians 3:20 NLT)

Clay

But now, O Lord, thou art the father; we are the clay, and thou our potter; and we all are the work of thy hand.

(Isaiah 64:8 KJV)

Earthen Vessels

But we have this treasure in earthen vessels, that the excellency of the power may be of God, and not of us.

(2 Corinthians 4:7 KJV)

Forgiven

If we confess our sins, he is faithful and just and will forgive us our sins and purify us from all unrighteousness.

(I John 1:9 KJV)

Free Indeed

*If the Son therefore shall make you free,
ye shall be free indeed.*

(John 8:36 KJV)

Friend

I no longer call you servants, because a servant does not know his master's business. Instead, I have called you friends, for everything that I learned from my father I have made known to you.

(John 15:15 NIV)

God's Own

The Spirit marks us as God's own. We can now be sure that someday we will receive all that God has promised. That will happen after God sets all of his people completely free. All of those things will bring praise to his glory.

(Ephesians 1:14 NIV)

Good Soldier

Endure hardship with us like a good soldier of Christ Jesus.

(2 Timothy 2:3 NIV)

Habitation of God

In whom ye also are builded together for an habitation of God through the Spirit.

(Ephesians 2:22 KJV)

Handiwork

For we are God's handiwork, created in Christ Jesus to do good works, which God prepared in advance for us to do.

(Ephesians 2:10 NIV)

Head

And the LORD shall make thee the head, and not the tail; and thou shalt be above only, and thou shalt not be beneath; if that thou hearken unto the commandments of the LORD thy God, which I command thee this day, to observe and to do them.

(Deuteronomy 28:13 KJV)

Heirs and Joint Heirs

And if children, then heirs — heirs of God and joint heirs with Christ, if so it be that we suffer with Him, that we may be also glorified together.

(Romans 8:17 KJV)

Holy

Because it is written, Be ye holy, for I am holy."

(I Peter 1:15 KJV)

Holy Nation

But you are a chosen people, a royal priesthood, a holy nation, God's special possession, that you may declare the praises of him who called you out of darkness into his wonderful light.

(I Peter 2:9 NIV)

Holy Temple

Do you not know that you are the temple of God and that the Spirit of God dwells in you?

(1 Corinthians 2:8 NIV)

Kings and Priests

And hath made us kings and priests unto God and his Father; to him be glory and dominion for ever and ever. Amen.

(Revelation 1:6 KJV)

𝔏ender

Lord shall open unto thee his good treasure, the heaven to give the rain unto thy land in his season, and to bless all the work of thine hand: and thou shalt lend unto many nations, and thou shalt not borrow.

(Deuteronomy 28:12 KJV)

Light of the World

Ye are the light of the world. A city that is set on a hill cannot be hid.

(Matthew 5:14 NIV)

Little One

Even so it is not the will of your Father which is in heaven, that one of these little ones should perish.

(Matthew 18:14 NIV)

Masterpiece

For we are God's masterpiece. He has created us anew in Christ Jesus, so we can do the good things he planned for us long ago.

(Ephesians 2:10 NLT)

Merciful

God blesses those who are merciful, for they will be shown mercy.

(Matthew 5:7 NLT)

Meek

Blessed are the meek, For they shall inherit the earth.

(Matthew 5:5 KJV)

Mine

Do not fear, for I have redeemed you; I have summoned you by name; you are mine.

(Isaiah 43:1b NIV)

More than Conquerors

No, in all these things we are more than conquerors through him who loved us.

(Romans 8:37 NIV)

My Little Children

My little children, let us not love in word, neither in tongue, but in deed and in truth.

(I John 3:18 KJV)

New Creation

Therefore if any man be in Christ, he is a new creature: old things are passed away; behold, all things are become new.

(2 Corinthians 5:17 KJV)

Overcomer

For whatsoever is born of God overcometh the world: and this is the victory that overcometh the world, even our faith.

(I John 5:4 KJV)

Peacemaker

Blessed are the peacemakers: for they shall be called the children of God.

(Matthew 5:9 KJV)

Peculiar

For thou art an holy people unto the Lord thy God, and the Lord hath chosen thee to be a peculiar people unto himself, above all the nations that are upon the earth.

(Deuteronomy 14:2 KJV)

Possession

For you are a people holy to the Lord your God. Out of all the peoples on the face of the earth, the Lord has chosen you to be his treasured possession.

(Deuteronomy 14:2 NIV)

People unto Himself

For thou art an holy people unto the Lord thy God: the Lord thy God hath chosen thee to be a special people unto himself, above all people that are upon the face of the earth.

(Deuteronomy 7:6 KJV)

People of His Pasture

For he is our God; And we are the people of his pasture, and the sheep of his hand

(Psalm 95:7 KJV)

Poor in Spirit

Blessed are the poor in spirit: for theirs is the kingdom of heaven.

(Matthew 5:3 KJV)

Redeemed

I have swept away your offenses like a cloud, your sins like the morning mist. Return to me, for I have redeemed you.

(Isaiah 44:22 NIV)

Remnant

Even so then at this present time also there is a remnant according to the election of grace.

(Romans 11:5 KJV)

Righteousness of God

God made him who had no sin to be sin for us, so that in him we might become the righteousness of God.

(2 Corinthians 5:21 NIV)

Royal Priesthood

But you are a chosen people, a royal priesthood, a holy nation, God's special possession, that you may declare the praises of him who called you out of darkness into his wonderful light.

(I Peter 2:9 NIV)

Salt of the Earth

You are the salt of the earth. But if the salt loses its saltiness, how can it be made salty again? It is no longer good for anything, except to be thrown out and trampled underfoot.

(Matthew 5:13 NIV)

Saved

*If you openly declare that Jesus is Lord
and believe in your heart that God
raised him from the dead,
you will be saved.*

(Romans 10:9 NLT)

Sheep

My sheep listen my voice; I know them, and they follow me.

(John 10:27 NIV)

Sons and Daughters

And, "I will be a Father to you, and you will be my sons and daughters, says the Lord Almighty."

(2 Corinthians 6:18 NIV)

Temple of God

Don't you know that you yourselves are God's temple and that God's Spirit dwells in your midst?

(1 Corinthians 3:16 NIV)

About the Author

Kandra Charlene Albury is an extravagant peacekeeper, servant leader, author, children's advocate, and business strategist. She is also the Co-CEO and Founder of More Than

Expected (MTE) Publishing, a full-service publishing and branding agency based in Gainesville, FL.

She earned a bachelor's degree in communication from the University of North Florida and a master's degree in mass communication from the University of Florida. She has a Ph.D. in ministerial education from Truth Bible University, and she is a proud product of the Putnam County

School System. She has more than 15 years of executive-level and [C-suite] communication experience.

Kandra is married to James C. Albury. They are honored to be the parents of three amazing children and an awesome grandson.

She is a member of Zeta Phi Beta Sorority, Inc. Gainesville's Delta Sigma Zeta Chapter.

When Kandra isn't serving in the Kingdom or coaching her clients, she is enjoying warm sunsets at nearby Florida beaches.

To learn more about Kandra and explore her work, visit her website: KandraAlbury.org

www.ingramcontent.com/pod-product-compliance
Lightning Source LLC
LaVergne TN
LVHW041225080526
838199LV00083B/3362